Clipped Wings
& Other Things
That Keep a
Bird
From Flying

Cover Art & Book design by Michael James Haley

First Paperback Edition: April 2023

ISBN: 979-8-9879452-3-0
eISBN: 979-8-9879452-4-7

Goldspin

~~For You~~
~~About You~~
This one is for Me.

Contents

Perfer et obdura, dolor hic tibi proderit olim.

Be patient, and tough;
    Someday this pain will be useful to you.

Ovid

Me with my hand outstretched, hoping someone
    will take it.

Aretha Franklin

Introduction
2018

Here's perched a bird inside of a cage,
A writer, lost when without their page,
No pen to pen, nor voice to sing,
Here lies a muted a muddled thing.

A puddle pooled from vagrant rains
Whose thunderstorms still rage in plains.
With roars of right, and claps of wrong
"To family is where you belong!"

Soon seeds of doubt from puddle sprout.
With hope, they may bloom some day
From wicked weed to flourishing flower.
As birdy sulks, all salt and sour

A Muse, amused, kicks off his shoes.

While Sparrow, caged, wing waves its rage
The muse, he knows it will be soon
That bird will find its cages key
Just beneath their raging wing.

Rose
2020

A rose was left in the sun.
It shriveled and died there.
The crimson petals wilted, and crisped
Some detached and traveled with the wind
Picking it up now, the entire bud falls away
But the thorns remain strong
Ready to defend their beauty.

Weathered

2017

5

I wish I knew the winds the way the earth does
That they molded me like ocean waves and shaped me like stone
I wish that I knew the rains as do temperate forests
And that the sun left me often to grow on my own
Twould be grand to be like sand tenderly built upon by hands
So gentle, even a shout too loud could tear this castle to the ground
If I could be like most plants and stretch my roots into the soil
Perhaps I would there find some friends that value me as if I'm oil
Instead, I'm more like tumbleweed, drifting on parched countryside
Desperate to find moisture wherever I can
And the wind tells of the ocean,
Of rains in the forest,
But carries me not past these dry barren lands.

Simple Stated Susan
2017

Simple Stated Susan goes perusing through the streets when she's
    been using
Self-abusing
Self-deluding
Always proving she's a nuisance with her two cents.
Always losing to the truth
Stays 'round a few men she'll never give it up to or choose
Tends to find herself in games she'll probably lose
Over comfortable in someone else's shoes,
She loves to hog all their views and make them her own
Unhappy when she's alone, but never stays around for long
Unless you're picking up or putting down while she
    sings you her song
Never missing high notes when the paintbrush is stroking long
Her body is a canvas for con artists to put coating on
Then go 'round boasting of how they just did ol' Susan wrong
While she, all unawares, picks up her panties and moves along.
She, much more aware than they could care to know
    puts on her show
Awaiting her own space to grow and watching for her place to go
Where every friendly face she knows is genuinely filled with hope
For someday pleasures, past endeavors teaching them
    what future holds
Could never measure them in treasures:
        Diamonds, Rubies, Minks, or Gold
But values valued often lesser, banks and hands cannot behold.
They don't get old since life is a fertile fountain full of wonder
Not a blunder sets those fragile hearts asunder
Don't be under the impression that their blessings are something to
    be plundered
That motivation sets deific clouds to thunder.

So, Susan wanders through the streets on calloused feet,
Remaining meek when life is bleak, and searching for her
    suitor sweet
He'll take her to that mountains peak where others like her
    wait to meet
And Simple Stated Susan will be praised for her complexity
And find her squandered life is no more threatened by its brevity

Brush Before Fire
2019

"I want to be ambidextrous." They said with bright eyes.
They were a peculiar dreamer, and that never did fade.
"I want to write with both hands and speak in eight languages
"Tell stories from them all,"
And still they dreamed on,
"I want an empire of creation,
"Golden-Spun tales from a House of my own
I want gelato in Rome, and Romance in Venice."
They had lofty ambitions. That never changed either
"I want to fight the good fight." They dreamed, a little older, high
on their youth and rebellious spirit.
"I want to stand with the heroes of my generation and join a
        revolution for the good of man
"With a pen in my hand, or from the microphone stand.
"I want to live forever just to see the world end.
"To witness the planetary migration of man."
He boasted on about big dreams and wishes, but, taken by life, also
        wished for lesser things:
The end of a shift
Good company
Peace of mind.
"I want to turn back time." He dreamed as he does.
"This life has ravaged me, but my spirit lives on,
A knotted, dry thing like brush before fire
All it needs is a spark to show the world how it burns.

Nearly Forgotten
Reflected across the train
Watching my self

Head lifted
Locked eyes
Determined

Soul-Eater
2017

It takes more than one condition to show me unconditional love
I lay the terms out in blood from this throbbing apple
       —Core of your vision
First, don't shadow my vision with any frames, filters, or fibbing,
But pile high the provisions that will feed my creative soul.
I roll with the rocks down a fretboard and into a hole
Ascending the scales of your highest mountain,
Striking into golden piano chords.
Feed my soul!

Consider feeding me yours.
Lead me on tours of your layered mind,
Following forking paths of your pulsing veins
Swinging from the vines of your tangled mane
Feed me your soul so that I might love you whole
From soft skinned chagrin to the stubborn jut of your chin,
And the furrowed frown of your brow over stormy eyes.
I'll give in if you would just
Feed my soul!
And I will roll with the rocks up a fretboard from a hole
Descending the scales of your highest mountain,
Striking into golden piano chords
Feed my soul
And then pressure that coal into a diamond you'll hold
From one knee, up to me
Proposing a love unconditionally.

Bleeding Art

2017

I offered one my tattered sleeve
Saliva soaked and torn apart
From stretched and shy pubescent cuff
I offered him my bleeding heart

I passed along that canvas, blank
And asked him not to make it art
For art is pain and everlasting
I asked him not to play his part

But art was made; his part was played
I wept as lovers weep when they do part
A masterpiece he left in pieces
On harpsichord he played my heart

Then sometime later, to another,
A beating heart, did I present
With hazy eyes, he said to me,
"There's beauty here in bleeding art

For art is joy, and art is pleasure
Pain is simply tax to treasure"
Then play my heart, he did as well
On catgut orchestrated swell.

For quite some time did I, then, hide
My shaded heart confined
Prose-paint pulsing pulmonary
Beating heart pumped my design

Clipped Wings

It bled my soul for red wine wisdom
Barrel aged and sweet berry tart
Bitter blues and robust flavors
On stolen palettes turned to art

Now when I cross another lover
Sultry seducer with art as well
I'll offer him a bleeding heart
Play his on drums, and never tell.

Timeless Love

I

He thinks that he can see me through how broken I am
My puzzle pieces, so worn and weathered, no longer fit together
Still, he swears he's seen this picture 7 billion times
It's no wonder when he views it through kaleidoscope eyes.

I'm more than pretty enough for him to hang on his wall
Leveling tilts from wrong to right so as to avoid the fall
Holding me centered in his eyes, he tries to frame me with his lies
But I'm too big for his frame of mind—
More than one night stand can hold as the clock ticks by his side.
If I slid out from under arms then I might do no harm
But the lonely air is cold from the beneath these blankets
I stay, letting his hands tickle time away
Into a love from yesterday.

II

Hours crawl backwards with my fingers over the rise and fall of
        his chest.
Breath, the crest of a wave he says I'm surfboarding best
I, much like the faithful on Sundays, met him here to confess to
        sinful feelings—
We promised there'd be no feelings.
Still, I'm reeling from his absences and parched from all
        this abstinence,
But finally, I have the sense to leave without the baggage
Since he has a whole commitment to fulfill that deals with
        me in the least
Yet has the nerve to say I fear what that commitment should mean.

Clipped Wings

The nerve it takes to accuse me of housing issues with trust
When that's the truth the most for him. My only problem is lust
Lust for the lump in those joggers, and the hump in his rear
For the tongue between teeth and whispered words in my ear.
Those ticklish jabs to my side, and playful pins to the wall
He's so aggressive and the danger had me craving the fall
And so, I tilt to the left, forget how wrong it may be
I always did prefer the floor with him looming over me.

III

Mr. Possessive really loved his independence.
Kept my heart in chains like pendants
Loved to punish me like penance
I confessed, here's my repentance:
Rent my heart out like a tenant
Pimp my heart out for his rent,
Leave me starved without a cent,
Exhausted.
All energy spent traversing fields in his head-games,
Running suicides on courts,
Jumping burpees trying to work out what he was training me for.
He asked if I enjoyed the coy way that he toyed with my mind
I admit that masochism never felt so divine.

A masochistic pacifist combatting blows with passive fists
They fire fatal for the win. I take their shots upon my chin.
Malicious smiles and greedy grins
I count to three. They have me pinned.
Come set me free!
Oh, referee!
I'm breaking free!

Too many times have I added to this pattern.
Each time I walk away, pride bruised, bloody-battered.
I step into the trap and catch my dagger in my back.

Let it glance off thicker skin and I will throw it back.
Guilty heart bleeding from the beating of a judge's heavy gavel
Love is akin to time-travel.

Bloodlust
2018

Lust
For red wine drips from fingertip
Drawn quick from a thorned crown placed on my head
Sample it before I am lain to bed
Full bodied and thick with disdain

Lust
For the scandal of my slender build
Vulnerable, posted display for the world.
Barter your envy for impotent fame
The bricks of my legacy placed

Lust
After darkness and circled blue eyes
Deep purple impressed from royalty's stamp
Meter my heart, but in measures of Amp
Electric beats pounding with grace.

Ah, "Lust"
Encapsulates hunger so deft
I'm starved for the challenge that few have yet made
Lust claws at my gluttony
Still, I must resist this tempting refrain.

Creep
2018

Here I sit watching you sleep—a creep.
Admiring peeking piglets poking from the bottom of a blanket that
    cascades over your slender frame in rippling red waves
You rest
       At peace
            I watch.

Here I sigh watching you lie to rest—my conquest.
Now faded lips, once tinted wine, were wedged between mine as
    our bodies thrashed wildly on whatever would catch, and
      then...
You sleep
      In peace
         I watch—a creep

Perched right here, watching you sleep, I creep
Nearer to lengthy butterfly lashes, hands splayed timidly towards
    an oozing concave of ragged gashes,
Red waves oozing from your head, cascading over lengthy lashes
    that once lifted to see me thrashing wildly on whatever would
      catch,
Splayed hands reaching for a wine bottle wedged, and then
    concaved your head...
You Rest
      In Peace
         I watch
               A creep

A Watched Pot
2021

One Grain of sand
    F.... ....F
     L.............L
      O.........O
       A.....A
        T.T
      I   I
     N . N
    G   G
Towards the depths
Nervous anticipation
Antagonizing patience
As I wait for another

          And wait...

              And wait...

It stirs forgotten hatred
A desert disdain
Inspires quaking hands to
Shake another pebble through
Flood it out with water
But that'd only muddy plans
Stop the time completely
So I sit
And wait
And watch
One grain of sand
Feather slowly to the bottom

The Watched Man

2018

Watched hands, they never move
But a watched man?
He moves too soon
The watcher tries, but held in time
It's tough to make his soon enough

The right time comes and passes, fleeting
Three watch hands at noon-time meeting
He sighs away his passing chance
Spellbound by the watched man

Watched hands, they never move
Unless those hands are the watched man's
He moves them, reaching for another
The watcher watches, longing

(C/F)uck
2021

It would have thrilled you to be aware
I was there,
flesh bare, and
pulling hair,
a witness to every thrust of your sword,
every javelin thrown,
each excruciating pass with your jousting pole.
I heard the cheers and the screams,
the handless clapping—
were you aware?
It must have thrilled you to have me there
pressed to cold walls,
and pleading
for you
to stop.

Slip & Fall
2017

Must be my sanity slipping that makes me think this is love.
To play the part of fool again for you is enough
To have me standing in line for my chance to bring you proof
Can't no other hold it down like I can do.
I try to keep an empty hamper:
Clothes folded and ironed
Vow to cater to my man when he comes through the door tired
If we could only procreate, I'd name them Destiny's Child
Guess all this wishful thinking is just me in denial

Shit

I'll put dinner on the table if you give me the label:
More than friends
Until the end
Death do us part
And no fables!
I want to curl up in your arms under the charm of your grey-blues
Those stormy skies in stormy eyes wear no disguise.
Let me play you a song on fine strands of your silky brown hair
Close the space between our lips so we can breathe the same air
If you just said you felt the same, then that would only be fair
But life's a bitch, and never this
So, I won't care.

I don't care about the way your face lights up when you're
        acting a fool
I'm only laughing at myself for being taken so soon
It doesn't matter if you flatter me by batting those lashes

Clipped Wings

Every flutter leaves a gash like flogging lashes
My repentance for the sin of flirty grins and glances under the brow
Yet I would do it all again if I could be with you now
I guess I haven't learned my lesson, and I'll do it again.
Slipping sanity making me love a friend
Between men.

I slip in slick from the sick that you make me feel
When you give my faith in God, but insist that he isn't real and
        when you
Give me feelings the world says I shouldn't feel
It's sanity that I'm slipping in
My sanity
Insanity

I slip in sanity when you gas up my vanity
Holding out helping hands just to take them back
Sends me tumbling, crumbling, spinning 'round
I'm such a bumbling fool
My heart is set to slip in wet and send me falling for you
I'm slipping, tripping, dripping tears and crippled from
        all the pain
You hold a light to all my fears and then you gas them with shame
It sends me reeling
My head in the ground repealing
The truth of what you aren't feeling
These moments that I keep stealing, I'm collecting to keep trying
        some more
And when my sanity puddles up on the floor
I slip and fall.

Madness
2021

Madness has settled in my feeble mind, be warned,
For as I stare deeply into your eyes
Admire the parabolic curve of your plump and puckered lips
I see in these your reciprical affection

You strike with correction
Indict for baseless desire
I charge you as a liar!
Delusion in full bloom.

Yet Thoughts Of You Still Loop Around.......

.......On Tracks Within My Sane Mind

Sanity Sands
2017

I rose and fell like the swell of the ocean,
Temperate water rushing away from eager toes.
I averted my eyes and skewed my devotion
With a thorny red rose that I held in my hands
As I fell in the swell of the ocean.

I had spent much time since my journey began
Constructing my fortress, all built out of sand
'Til the wave came upon me,
That conquering swell
To the western most ocean I fell.

Waves beat rhythms into my ears
I broke each one with a desperate swim
Salt water filled my eyes to the brim
As I rose and I fell in that furious swell
I fear I may have died as well.

When I woke again on dryer land
My fortress grand was naught but sand
Disolven in that ocean swell
Upon my knees I fell.

I start to build my fortress grand
Again, and once more out of sand
I build it fast and sturdy strong
Raise the drawbridge; seal it quick
There's sure to be another swell
Bet this time I'll do twice as well.

Little Running Bear
2019

Such a poignant name,
Little Running Bear,
Since I hunger for the honey,
And go sprinting toward the swarm
Where I feast upon their nectar
With my skin too thick for stinging.
I do hunger for the honey,
But I'm starving for the pain,

And so, what a poignant name,
Little Running Bear.
Like a moth gone to the flame
I go chasing after honey,
And the nectar is never mine,
So, they swarm me, and they're stinging,
But I only taste the honey.
I've grown numb to all of the pain.

It always seems so kind
That they share the nectar with me,
But they're always baring stingers;
Endless dives to bring me pain,
So, I'll leave them to their fury,
Take off hunting for more honey,
And so, what a poignant name,
Little Running Bear.

Even Icarus
2019

Even Icarus could not resist.
Though the sun singed his feathers
Though hot wax dripped and blistered his skin
Even he could not deny his desire to fly higher.

So how could I
Knowing well
I'll fall the same
One way or another.

Rivers Fall
2019

Rivers fall hard into pools of faith
Sing sweet serenity in the bottom of a brook
And they do rage down mountains in cascade
Roaring on for miles

I also used to roar that loud.

I still do fall like rivers
At the ends of earth where no pool waits
Only the luminous blue of space and starlight
I love to swim there too.

Tidal
2021

If I should become distracted
Know that I've only become so
Identifying the contours of your body
Through ripples in your jeans.
Hypnotized by the rhythmic swell of
Blood flowing through your veins
Tendon and sinew pulsing in the convex of your neck.
Notice how the proximity affects us both
Your racing heart challenges mine
I'm out of breath before the pistol starts.
Permit me to catch it in your hair
Once your eyes have washed over me
And I'm left tumbling in the current
Somersaulting ashore
I'll take my sandlot kisses
Been known to steal a base or two
And you...
        And you...

The Water is Fine
2020

It was almost in his hands, but he only grazed my heart
Bloodied only the tips of his fingers
Like testing the waters in a swimming pool
Dipping a toe in ocean waves, early summer
He almost had me then

I habitually submerge my head in the shallows of love
False as it is. The job is always done well:
I no longer hear logic or reason.
My heartbeat echoes like that of a child in ultrasound
Accelerated and panicked at the unfamiliar sensation

I want with an infantile dependence
It is quite frightening, I imagine. Who wants to be
responsible for such frailty?
I need with the fervor of a sobering addict who never moved
        through the first step.
"I am not in love with…"

I am not married to the idea of myself,
But cycle through masks like colors on a mood ring.
The ones I like best are painted and docile
I gestate behind them to fill the changing molds

True comfort lies behind broken masks.
Those of stone and waterlogged wood,
The most worn, cracked and aged into grimace and scowl.

I ride on them like rafts to keep from drowning in the waters,
But habitually submerge my head in the shallows of love.

Eye of the Beholder
2018

She glanced at the reflection in a puddle from unyielding rains
Disgusted, she saw every chiseled flaw:
The sockets rubbed raw
The un-aligning jaw
The bulbous nose about lips of rose
Shielding rows of jagged stones
A furrowed brow plucked too thin now
The frown lines and worry wrinkles.
Her eyes behold no beauty, only the harshest scrutiny.

She once created art on a worn and tattered canvas with a palette
        of clay and mud
She dipped her brush in war-paint,
Buffed it into porcelain
Powdered that with cocaine
Until only she could recognize the pain hidden therein.
All the surveyors cried,
"Mutiny! Mutiny! Mutiny!"
Scrutiny.

One million times or more she's stared too briefly into
        sapphire oceans,
Sunlight bursting through branch hazeled leaves,
Silver steel shining through tarnished clouds,
And amber honey glistening in decadent chocolate.
She takes fleeting looks into one million eyes or more
Wonders what they see, with her own cast to the floor.

Perfection?
Suspection?
Scrutiny?

Ray
2018

Emerald hills alight with fire, burning in your eyes.
Reflections of my desire flicker on the flames.
Glowing in the dim lit night,
A smoldering gaze sets me alight.
I burn in the emeralds of your eyes
Intent to make my claim

Arrows from a winged bow whisper by keen ears,
Glinting in the fiery glow, feather ends caressing
Shower me with unheard wisdom
Flurries of seductive nothings
Can't help but lean in to hear
The passion you're expressing.

Shower me in gasoline to catch the fire of your eyes.
Emerald flames on a swaying frame, flickering seduction
Tracing fingers send embers flying
A smoldering kiss so gratifying
I burn in the emeralds of your eyes
Intent to scorch my claim.

Chance
2021

We played the same 16 in a row
Waged our war like Rochambeau
The likelihood is slim, I know
Who could plan such serendipity

The Matador

Particles

2021 - 2022

Matador I
Suerte De Capote

Regard me now in my querencia
This you cannot take from me
Regard me in my prideful saunter
Catch the clip of my hooves—
Dancers in the bullring—
Wish I'd never caught your movements in the corner of
my eye.

Regard me now
Before the Picadors have ruined me
And you've tired me with your lances
Flaunting fair Veronica
And the crimson cascades to paint us in matching dress
And you've shown them all your power
Ravaged my humility
Pulled your cape too many times
Proved you're never on the other side
And I'm tired
And I'm hurt,
And I'm broken
And I've bowed in defeat.

Regard me now,
Matador!

Matador II
Tercio De Varas

Matador, Matador
What is it you tease me for
I track your movements long before you wave your tattered kerchief.
Like a fool,
I charge towards the challenge

Matador, Matador,
What expressionist modes do you model for
With each passionate pose, I charge forward
To snag my horns—
Like a fool—
    on canvas
And cover my face in paints.

Your irons do not pain me, nor dissuade me, dearest Matador
I should find myself discouraged every time you dance away,
But, impassioned by your challenges, I love you still and evermore.
Can't see you paint me all in red,
My sweetest Matador.

Matador III
Picador

Pick up the sound, Picador
And turn your heart another way
What foolish knight wins wars on blinded steeds?
What cowardice might inspire another needless slaughter?

Dearest Picador,
Hear my heart
And spare me the lances
Clod on back behind the bullring fences
Flee the sound of my hoofbeat
And see how the Matador bloodies your hands
Throws you to a death before him to measure my rage
That mattress guard may shield the gore
But can you dodge my lethal horn?
This needless fight was never yours
Sweet Picador, do spare me.

Matador IV
Tercio De Muerte

I bow to your craft, Matador
Even my bullish nature cannot contend.
How the stubborn bone in my brow offends,
Yet fails to defend my open heart
Do it quickly!
You and the Picadors have had your fun,
I've danced with you all on this mission for one.
What a fault I've made
Do it quickly, please.
I've grown too weary of this bullring sun.

Having lost myself in your desert mirages
I concede my defeat and leave you my heart
Many times, did I charge forth, deluded by your phantoms
Only to find you'd danced away
Surely towards another
Will you ravish your new lover the way you've ravaged me?
Do it quickly, sweet Matador.
Quickly, and clean.
Have mercy on this ragged heart
I bow, now, to your craft

Matador V
Gore/The Bull Wins

Regard me now
A ragged mess
Deflated chest, and
The Gore
Do you think you have me?
Are there concessions made in this labored breath?
My head is not yet bowed, tread carefully my sweet
So eager now to see my heart
After I've given so much chase
And your endless dance-aways
Arrogant passes with your dancing cape
Should I greet you sweetly with a yielding bow?

Matador

The name remains for both to claim,
Do you think you have me?
Go on then, step forward
Peek at my despairing heart
See the torn and bloodied canvas of my being.
Is this the art you sought to create?
The visceral pain of a tortured love
The tragic irony of a thin, cowardly man
Dismantling the beast that loves him so
Is this the art?
A comedy, only if we wed in the end.
Go on then, step forward.
Do you think you have me?
I'll bow to your craft—step sweetly now—
Lower, even, just for you
Do you think you have me still?

Can you see me through the gore?
See there nestled in the flesh
My heart is still beating.
One step more
In the eyes now where the embers still burn.
Can you see it?
That lingering rage;
My lingering love?
Now feel the greatness of my horn in your heart, ran through.
This bull was bound to win.

Fin.

Shades of You/
My Favorite Palette
2019

I could lie in bed
thinking of you
all day long
when the sky is gray
with rain clouds,
Thoughts of you
happy Yellow glow
to light my nights
illuminate my life
and guide me,
I can dip myself
into your fountain
submerge my sword
and fill my soul
with Blue,
Like I feel
near the ocean
waves crashing
drowning fears and
masking tears,
One day I'll
trace the shape of
your lips
with my tongue
from memory,
Shades of Pink
flowering there
bloom into Reds
and soft Purples,
I kneel at the throne,
My heart

where you reign
preserved on canvas
in Shades of You
paint from My Favorite Palette

Ray 4
2019

Do you know the way I see you,
The way I saw you then
When darkness drifted in
Heavy motes along my floor?

"Come to me," I implored,
Pleading for your presence.
You stood in brilliance at my door.
Even the sun could not contend.

Even the sunlight in my window
Became molten into darkness
Feeding shadows all dissolven
Into motes along my walls,

But when you stood in my door,
For the briefest of all times,
Not a shadow could withstand you.
Tell me where it is you go

When you leave me to the darkness
I'll pretend I never know
Because knowing brings the shadows
And I much prefer the glow.

Ray 11
2020

47

I think of you often
I think of introductions in a fated commune
I called you by my name
You called me by yours
I think of pillow talks on pillow walks
Of thrift shops for winter tops
I think of you often
If I don't think of you always.

I think of glowing orange in a donut shop
The hysterical laughter at the brilliance of it all
Even Dunkin laughed, though he couldn't have known—
Couldn't guess at the monkey on the mountain, all alone
Or the writhing mounds of old thanksgiving feasts
The psychedelic feats achieved.

I think of nut-butter fudge covered pretzels
And swirls of the same in sweet vanilla cream
Of waffle cut wafers with caramel in between
Bringing you sweets to make you sweet on me
And I should think of you nevermore
Still, I think of you, nonetheless.

A thumb war veteran happy to hold hands,
Determining a win if the game is in your eyes
Where the emerald hills burn.
I see that you still yearn for
Whispered wants over Uncut Gems,
Muddled terms of endearment.
A dive, head first into Union Pools
Hardly douses flickering flames

Clipped Wings

You traced the curve through every sway
I noticed, and even still replay
 Our night lost in Oasis,
Subject of my Wonderwall
You may not think of me at all
But I do think of you often
If I don't think of you always

Magnetic
2014

Diamond smile, hypnotic eyes
How you stir the butterflies
Wish chasing you was not so hard
Still, I have faith in magnetic hearts.

March of the Monarchs
2021

The way he dropped butterflies into my gut
        —Coins into the bank of a pig
Made me wonder if he planned some grand release
A march of the monarchs toward hydrangea inflorescence
Or sought to counterbalance the alarming velocity of my enamor
That I might feather safely to the floor
But the buoyancy of an elated heart carries me skyward
And my gaseous thoughts spread wildly throughout
A cumulus cloud of collected recollections
Imagined futures spun from present day premonitions,
The image of a face awash with grief
Showering over proverbial gardens
Salting the soils of my mind

The way he dropped butterflies into my gut
So that they might flock to the flora,
I thought
I feared
I knew that he might
Turn up the earth at my feet and reacquaint me with the madness
But that a bed of fresh soil would be made for us
Where we would lay, and burrow, and fight madly together
Opening holes to deliver our seed
Nourish our soil and grow our garden
Giving these cursed butterflies a home.

Steel
2020

Your eyes cut like steel with no wound left in wake,
Stomach set aflutter; monarch wingbeats stirring nerves
See how I look up at you, wide-eyed and pleading
And how you look back down at me, sultry-eyed and needing
Excite me with a fingered bass,
Drumstick beating on my face
I bob my head in rhythms, but I let you choose the pace.

Tilt & Rhythm
2022

My head tilts side long
Longer than the longing in your eyes
Further than the dusty drawl of my whispered name
Sultry syllables surpassed only by time—
Those savory seconds slipping with each inch you slide
Closer to the soft lipped saunter from ear-lobe to collar
Firm tongues tender push against a pulse pumping from
      palpitating heart
My head tilts side long as you dive in for feeding.

As you dive in for feeding, my mouth agape,
Air grows damp from passion pleated breaths
Back-tilted head bobbing to the beat of a pelvic pound
I greedily embezzle from deposits you make
Drinking from the fountain as though siphoning youth
A sip from the hose takes me back to my youth
To the bruise sore knees, and snotted nose
I now favor play when we've shed all our clothes
Backward tilting, mouth agape
My head bobs to the beat of a pelvic pound
And with tender tongue, I measure

Any Hole's a Goal

Bromies, Brojobs, and Bromosexuals?

No Homo,

But I have the weirdest Broner right now!

Pillowcase

54

Thank you
For leaving your scent
I'd rather not give chase
I'll keep you here sidelong.

Digital Delude
2022

Could I seduce you this way?
From afar,
Only bars,
Only blue-light scripture
Not even a picture
Lest it's spun from these words
Lit by character fixtures
Symbolic characters revolting
Against cowardly strictures

Should I seduce you this way?
Over time
Ignoring crime
Choose to blood-let my resentment
Bleed you out for your repentance
Lest you remedy somehow
Take a pill for self-amendment
Maybe overdose on empathy
You may never regain sympathy

To woo me once more
Wound on a spool
A finger-fool
Tapping eagerly impatient
Rise and wonder where the days went
Swiping dreams for absoliution
Left for Hope, Right for Confucius
Trading thoughts for grande polution
Blindly braving devolution.

REMisce Lucidity
2023

The morning comes
to wake and find

Nights waste away on loving

You
do not
exist.

Odie Blues II
2022

Not a true blue
A lifeless pallid blue
Waxy and wan in slumber

An almost blue
But milky muted blue
Lips that may not speak again.

A powdered sky blue
Lightened hue blue
The draining warmth has left behind

A frost-bitten blue
Lost mitten blue
Fingers that my not touch again.

I feel the cool of it in my marrow
And the chill of it in my heart.
I'll still wait for you to keep me warm
Do not go gentle...
Do not go

A Walk in the Sun
2022

Come with me.
Leave the shadows to their heat chasing misery
The warmth has fled and waits for you on brighter sides
Stop stepping on the cracks with broken backs and empty stares
Hunched beneath the weight of a world wide sorrow
Aren't you cold there where the sun neglects?
The shivers and quakes of your body give way to such soul
    shaking sobs.
Are you miicking the rain?
You dark, hovering cloud wetting the ground.

Step with me now to the other side—
      —A brighter side
Where silver linings shine in radiant light
And warmth might see your tear puddles gone dry.
Here where heavens stand on earth with golden pillars
And the cracks we walk are not trenches to fall into
Not bottomless voids, but gardens, lush and green.
There is a beauty in living, even among the weeds
Come with me for a walk in the sun.

Closets
2022

No more twisting handles to bolted doors!
Brittle bones quake behind skins in the closet.
Fickle minds ache from computing absolution.
Dare to rob the sought-out treasures?
Gold is rarely given.
Draw the curtain; curtail pleasures.
Recall what has been striven for.

Password required at closet doors!
Rumors of trust earn fallacy rights
Skeletons within harbor speakeasy confidences.
Dare to donate shattered faith?
Gold may just repair.
Filling cracks to mend the wraith,
Product may compare.

Opposites Attract
2020

How fitting it is for me
To want you
When you don't want me at all,

As for her
Pursuit of me
As I'm chasing after you

I suppose it is true
This opposite attraction.

If Only For One
2022

Love is a thing that exists in but a moment
Not a myth, but a fleeting verity in distrust
An ironic isolate of bond building banter
It comes, lingers briefly, dashes on again
And then the gray
And then the quiet
And then bitter vicissitudes
Indignity spoils spilling deprecate pressure
Engine steam fragrant with betrayal and disdain
A damn burst bleeds the line with lust
Every touch
Every thrust
Every ardent bruise from overbearing holds lingers longer,
Still, It's not quite
Never just the same as that famed and fleeting feeling.
Yes, Love is a thing that exists, but
In a moment

It doesn't mean I love you less
Rather that I love me more

Why Bother?
2023

I've heard it all before
Some knock is at my door
But all that one could offer
I can give me plenty more
Youthful games are now a bore
Favor gentlemen to boors—
Why bother kiss them for?
I've already kissed the floor.

Focus
2020

Fickle minds can never do it. Flitting about like fruit flies feeding on fermented fig; sun drunk in the summer and fall

Oscillating ocular organs bouncing around from subject to subject—These eyes are had only for the one, but they like to keep their options open.

Can any blame be placed for it? Careless concentration is fleeting for both. The eyes can only watch, absent and distracted as all prior days' work is effortlessly

Undone by the temptation of superficial trophies; Undermined by the vagrant heart and fickle, fickle mind. Uncouth and uncanny, how easy it is to act against one's own

Self-interest, which advises surrender; a complete sacrifice of every subject if only for the sake of securing the trophies that matter

Focus on something more than the failures. Focus on more than the potential thereof. Focus on ribbons and medals for the small wins, and when the big win comes, focus only on the ones who never lost **FOCUS**.

Ode to Pen

2022

To my dearest friend,

How easily I forgive you,
Though you know all my secrets
And spill them here on page,
Mocking me plainly in thinly veiled rhetoric

You know I understand.
Others may only guess at your meaning, but
I see your intent,
Your tendency to ruin.

Sure,
I may pull the pin on hand grenades,
Lob them blindly over my shoulder;
I give little regard to where the shrapnel lands
Because you, too, regardless
Work with universal fervor.

If the wound is borne by many
Then the bomb was meant for all
Targeted or not.

What a dreadful burden you carry
And so the friendship must be true
In that you bare that weight of my heavy hand,
My heavy heart,
And my heavy mind,
Bloodletting only your own
On empty battlefields lined with curious anticipation;
On empty canvas awaiting the pools,

And how I must repay you in the only way I can:
By filling the fountain with my ancient soul.

So this one is for you
Oh, sweetest friend
With all my love
Ode to pen.

Exchanged Words
2021

Like the tickling of high ivories
Secrets and slander traveling lightly on the wind.
False confidences on unstable scaffolding
Misplaced intentions gone rogue in desire

Salted rains play percussive rhythms
Wronged winds weep in modulated whinnies
Truths long etched in cemented suspicions
Erode into falsehoods
From the tickling of high ivories
Secrets and slander traveling lightly on the wind
Calumny sediment poisoning water
And misplaced intentions gone rogue in desire.

Voices
2021

Though true that voices speak
You may not know the truth you seek
For voices speak in lies as well
So, who are they to tell

Thespian
2021

Not every thespian is an actor
Some village criers are only liars
And your platitudes do not go unheard
The slip-ups in your reveries do never go unnoticed
If you thought it so, then the Oscar goes to
Me.

Better Seasons

Do not wonder at the reason
When they've moved on to better seasons
And left the weight behind
Of a verdict doled to man untried
Such a man can only play the fool for measured time
And when midnight comes
You'll see a man
No more.

Wonderlands
2022

Tell me of the beauty that you find here in the winter
I tend to hide away when every warmth has left by mid-december
Yet you insist that wonderlands exist over the threshold
I may just trust that dream if you would carry me there..

When I step out on my own to see the glitter of a frost you promised
Browning mounds and muddied sloshes
Sock soaking, and toe biting, and feet sliding into shin deep traps
Am I to stay locked like this, frozen forever?

Describe the burn you feel on warmer days
Under scorching suns you to turn to run
From brighter sides for cold, frigid, snow-pregnant skies
If maddening gray is all you know
I'll teach you not to run from growth

Sweet prefacing petrichor
anticipating spring precipitations
Dew damp blades licking between toes
And the fragrant sweet roses—
Hydrangea blossoms bundled and bobbing in Madison Square
Soft winds feathering over ocean shores
Over the emergent trees whose just growing leaves
Ripple and dance in waves of their own
Tune into vibrant birdsong bravado emanant from
Returning flock; feather filled canopies

Turned ahead clock to greet the longer days
What winter beauty could match it?
Tell me
I'll wait.

This is a fight that keeps with you

So long as you keep on keeping on

War Has Never Been This Way
2021

The beautiful things.

Butterflies and songbirds aflutter over tulip blooms and
    willow trees
Ever taking root in the soils of my mind
Ever trapped in waging war against the countertide

And beauty can draw blood

Willow ensnared by blackberry rose,
Drawn by thorn and bramble
Glinting mosaic from lunging serpents
Ever lost in battles of their own
Always gripping too tightly
Nearly impossible to hold on to themselves

War has never been this way
But hasn't it always?

To the blown bulbs that kept US in darkness
For lighting another path towards liberation
To the false faithful fires they burned in our yards
Only tinder to fuel the flames in our hearts,
Raise a glass
To those disturbed by the warmth we can conduct even in their
    harshest winters
To the deep baritones and soul digging saxophones
To the hymns hummed on railroads

War has always been this way

Clipped Wings

For the delighted Fae flittering about plum trees
Living freely is a threat to our survival
So we douse our wings in glitter and flitter harder in protest
Blinding with our brilliance
Taunting miserable fools who bind themselves in chains
How they do envy us even of our oppression.
And the war wages on...

Of the Klan
2021

Chase him down and spin him round
The circle is complete, my darlin
Loop him low, and deal the blow
He's dizzied on his feet, now. Quick!

We'll drink him good and don the hood
Make sure he doesn't peak
I bet he'll never know our colors well
To know that we compete

He'd never recognize our feet
From all this stomping in the mud
Or know the leader of our Cultish
Klan once painted in his blood

Long live the king, my brethren
All hail our father, true
Praise, now, our chief Grand Wizard
See the gift we've brought for you.

Surpassed Master
2021

Let the wisdom show now in the silver of your hair
And the entrenched leather of your aging face.
A master should know to demonstrate it best
With the occasional seat in a disciple's chair.

Let a true flower grow from the false seeds you've sown
But you can claim no credit for the garden you tend
Where the weeds ensnare and the pests consume,
And as many as you've grown, you've brought to their end.

Your petulant pesticides have poisoned your soils,
Now parched and dry like artistry malnourished
Have a seat, old friend. Let the wisdom flow on
You have burdened yourself with this weight for too long.

And see how it has made you!
More bitter than sweet,
Less gallant than creep,
And too blind to see that the children you've fostered,
All caring,
          All daring
Are craving destinations where you claim to lead
Only misleading.

How the high must have felt on the dawn of this journey
All strength and influence; young, hopeful and wild
But after eighteen years, have you grown from this, "Master"
Or only regressed to be more like a child?

Heir to None
2021

Heir to no nation
Claim to no throne
Swagger in untied shoes
Tripping on frayed powers
Undeserving yet entitled
It is but a feeling
Such rule does not extend here
Cannot be measured by a measure
To the height of crowning pinnacle
Nor compare to majestic mountains
What peaks the summit must descend
Willing and resentful
Unwilling and enraged
Ebb and flow of tidal waters
Surf the crest of waves ashore
Tumble to the coastline
Return to heaven,
Crownless
Retrun to sea
A king no more.

Waking Dream
2018

Fake battles in our hometown
Create wars all around
Counting sheep as their blown from the ground
By fake bombs touching down

Fake battles in our hometown
Bodies dancing to the sound
Of bassline bombings shaking the ground
And high hats firing tri-puh-let rounds.

Fake bullets fill our newspaper-down
Bed and blankets on the ground
Detonations blowing shrapnel around
Wide awake, but we keep our heads down.

Fake service when they tell us get down.
Hands raised to the sound
Of clicked-cock, pop, and gun hammer pound
Bleeding out, we're on the ground

Fake kindness when they're scared, they've been found
Off of their guard from the pistol redound
Fake battles have me wandering around
Asking for pinches. Could you please wake me now?

WMG

2018

Rain pit-patters on a classroom window
Clouds darken as madness approaches
Hear the panes rattle in their frames as the door swings open
Now the storm has arrived.

See the glass shatter, and the first blood splatter on a desktop
Cool air meets warmth spreading through chests
Classmates erupting in a whirlwind of fear
Are those rain drops, or tears in their eyes?

Thrown off balance, the world starts to spinning
Fall to the floor amid screaming winds
Rain drops climb a treacherous crescendo
The cold must have turned them to hail

The biting chill spreads from finger to toe
Vision slowly edged out by darkness
School is not time for sleeping, although
A storm's lullaby will always prevail.

Dreams of screams and showers of bullets
Wound in the chest that never does heal
A one man army only vaguely known
Eclipsing light in a tunnel of black

They wage their war in furious masks
No one recalls ever seeing them smile
Who knows where their rage is directed
          — Or if mentally affected
But where'd they gain access to weapons like that?

Straight for the Bullet
2020

Releasing a trigger does nothing once you pull it
What happened to electric charges?
Man, I ain't even hear no charges before you went
Straight for the bullet.

My ethnic history razed,
And now you're crying foul because your precinct is ablaze
We'll make our country greater once we send yours to the grave
Since you've forgotten how to tase,
Nah, you go
Straight for the bullet

Fascism on display.
White noise screaming
"Race, rats, race!"
Toe down on tail holding my race in place,
And more white noise laughter:
"It's a race rat race!"
Runners on their marks,
Keep those splayed hands raised,
Get set! He's g—
Go!
Straight for the bullet.

Tired arms from past times cracking that whip, huh?
Cramped up hands from all that nightstick grip, huh?
Water jetting hard from heavy hose, try not to trip.
"Arms tired? I better lighten up this clip."
Straight for the bullet.

Resolve
2020

At first it is all gold and silver.
The bridge is gold at Heaven's gates as we sail under to the
    Island of Angels
Golden summer hills surrounding,
The steel towers that we see from Ellis are silver in the sunlight,
Like the lining of the seafoam that carries us to shore
Where it becomes clouds fluffing up and around from below,
Boasting of the nation from a divine pedestal.
All silver, and gold
Majestic mountains, and amber waves, and
Emerald
She guides us into harbor with her raised torchlight,
Never slowed by the weight of broken shackles, and we are many
Our plights are many
Our resolve must be One.

Liberty and Opportunity, they promised us
Until we came to collect.
Now, we see that there is no gaud to the colors here
That was only the sun in our eyes
The golden hills are browning, burning, and dead.
The seafoam recoils from garbage shores.
There is naught but the silver of foil in blankets laid out for our
children in prison cells.
The only promise fulfilled is an involuntary liberation from family—
No!
There is no gold here anymore,
But the blue, white, red—
We had our revolution there too—
The red necks, the blue lives, the purest of whites,
And the brown.

Clipped Wings

Brown like the ground they sleep us in.
Black, and brown like the caked mud from our spilt blood.
We are the brown
And we are many.
Our plights are many
But our resolve *must* be One

The ivory whites live luxurious lives on the spoils of our labor
And when the meager pay is too much to bear
They send the work home.
Home to the places we flee.
Home to the places they dragged us from.
Lured us from with their baubles and gaud
We have found no freedom here
Chained to the guilt of the oppressor.
Waving our red, white blue, but like the Blue, White, Red,
We'll have our Revolution here too.
We are many.
Our plights are many.
Beware our single resolve.

Tiananmen Man
2023

It's a sign of the times
Droves of people wait in line
Drive to madness, faking fine
On their blue-light screens
Lies hardly seen

Forced to their confinement
Ration out subscribed consignments
Pay with life for useless signs
Plea your first degree
Earns pedigree

A massacre on either hand
Enslaved, or Tiananmen Man
All gather now to make a stand
Take to the Square
To make it fair

Gripping blue-light candles
Surveilant blades mishandled
They'll televise the scandal
Come to the square
Salvation is there.

Big Brother/Big Sister 84
(Boys and Girls Club)
2021

Boys and Girls all over town
Are stalking me
They're watching me

Red lights blinking all around
Hands up, eyes down
No stopping.

Brothers, Sisters all through town
Watch over me
Keep watch on me

They roll the tape and take me down
For all to see
Keep watching

Who should fear Big Brother now?
All of the brothers
Watch and see

Sisters too are on the prowl
You're canceled now
Who's watching

Boys and girls
All through the town
Make specatacle for all to see

Five eyes to a phone, head down
Watch out for me
I'm watching.

Big Brother/Big Sister 84
(Boys and Girls Club)
2023

Who should fear________________

____

____

____

____

Who's watching?

Boys and girls
All through the town

____

____

____

____

Boys _____________________
_____stalking_____

____

Red lights_____________________

____

___stopping.
_______________Sisters_______________
Watch_________
_________________me
______roll the tape________________________

____

____

In Appropriation
2019

Come in your nativity
My tongue does not spin gold
Their tales, half true, and tall indeed
Your histories hardly told

Bring forth your nativity
That I may know the world
Their simulacrums worn and bland
To brave your truth is bold

Teach me in your native dance
My feet don't know your rhythms
Their formulaic cadences
Make free-express forbidden

Bring to me your heritage
I have no plans to steal
I yearn to know a world exists
Outside of theirs that's real

So, speak to me in native verse
My tongue does not spin gold
I long to know the voice of those
Whose stories go untold.

Curious Cultivation
2019

Kingless kingdoms abound in timeless fields we plow
Castles of our intellect on mountains of our prowess.
Crowns are passed in fragments hand to hand among masters
May we feast upon their harvest, so no mind is left unfed.

The fruit of our existence held in word woven baskets
Water pumped from wells of wisdom nourish golden gourds,
And grow the sprouts of curiosity to jungles of our knowledge.
Pass our feast down, hand to hand, to leave no mind unfed.

Studious provisions of such worth are quick to spoil
And we are of such power, we can rot them with a phrase
Duteous preservation as we build upon our bounty
And pass our feast down, hand to hand, to leave no mind unfed.

Bored
2020

What a deafening silence
It is to be so...

Bored
Bored of the walls we live in
Bored of the day in, day out
Can't go out
Can't look forward
To another day of being
Another day of:
Political turmoil
Social unrest
Centuries old tensions
Simmering on high
And hasn't it made us

Bored
Bored of the incessant fight
Growth stunting blight
Black versus white
Only Black or White
Forgetting the spaces in between
Forgetting the childhood—
Dream of Unity!

Birds of Paradise
2017

Painted rainbows on a clear sky spectrum every vibrant color
Even Blu Jays and Red Robins know enough that they are brothers
And the yellow-necks and Greenbacks form a sisterhood of lovers,
Most who flee the winter's white-out,
Come to muddle out their colors.

Still, there's beauty there in snowy doves, and swans on lakes of ice.
Filter through oppressive noise and find that their songs, too, suffice
When up among clouds dancing, don't be frightened of the heights.
Hold the truth before your eyes:
We are all of Paradise

Miami-Dade
2020

Paradisiacal

When the girls flock in neon bright
Bikini tights
And I
Feign belonging
With neon-colored nails.

When green palms mingle with
Green plastic
Basket plants
Teal blue ocean
Waves to shore
And cruise ships
Idle on the horizon.

Paradise,
Where parasailers polka-dot
The waning summer skies

Where two men lift kettlebells
Beneath an overpass
And several underpasses later
Many more,

Homeless humans
Strewn across the pavement
Like the littered bottles,
Take out tins, and
Infectious masks
That accompany them.

Good morning!
One calls to me,
Or good afternoon!

Yes,
I chuckle

Good afternoon
I confirm.

How do you even find out anymore?
She asks to my
Waning summer smile.

I like your hat!
I like your tat!
I keep walking
Wishing for something
More substantial to offer.

I find myself
Or half of me, at least
In the streets of Overtown
Run down
Impoverished communities
Live in silent, eerie squalor.
Walk through bare pandemic streets where

More homeless humans lay
Strewn across the pavement
Like the littered bottles
Take out tins, and
Infectious masks
That accompany them in

Third World America

Covid-192020

It is a new world now.

Criminal plastic bags scuttle like ghost town tumbleweed.
The city that never sleeps turns restless in forced slumber
A quelled spirit boils in dark alleys and the underground
Threatening to resurface.

Will pressure release slowly through manhole covers
Oozing old-fashioned grime to reclaim familiar avenues?
Will it burst forth violently, snaking from abandoned stations
Coiling at the base of steel pillars in protest?
A demolition could be halted by eagles perched on Capitol Oak
Why choose, instead, to toss us down for feeding?
Plagued rats we must be.

Covid-192021

This is but the beginning
The dawn of an era
A new age of abundance
Of denial in excess
That access denial
Fueling the self-important
Unmasked patrons served by masked butlers,

Bid farewell to familiar faces
Become acquainted with the gaze
Longing yet untrusting
Piercing and revelatory
Adapt to the self-induced haze
Magnificent Hedone entwined with Algea
Anesthesia binds to keep doctors at bay
To keep the filth in their place
Steeping all the swine in mud
And the plagued rats should drown in grime
And the plagued rats were told many times
Still, dodging their shots
As though faced with a rite
So, deny in excess now
And hoard the access
It is our God given right!

This disease may meet its maker
To be followed by another
Perhaps this one won't remiss
And they'll deny in excess
Cling ravenous to their access
As it keeps them important

And the plagued rats should drown
And the plagued rats be drowned.

Extravagant Swine
2021   (I Hope My Black Skin Dirts Your White Tuxedo)

It's me!
The plagued rat left to drown
And the unmasked patron, yet
Indeed, also the rodent swine
Left rolling in the grime
Dear Algea, Hedone time!

It is me who chooses pain for pleasure
Dodging the extravagance
Though the ease of access tempts
And shouldn't I succumb one day
To the exclusive ball
And abundant denial would be cast from lips I own
Such a compelling power to wield
And still, I'll claim swine
What if I wield in rodent favor this time?
What then if we muddy their marble halls,
Stain their carpets and topple their walls
Strip down their gowns for our own masquerades
And bind them in chains for a game of charades?
Can't they see what we play at?
Are they not entertained
When the oppressed have become the oppressor off stage
Not scripted lies on a screen, but true life not seen before.
They've had centuries to pillage
Only a fool would give them more.

Writers Weild
2021

Stick and Stone may break the bone
Words often wound like cavalry
We save the blade for more violent days
Use ink to pen the calvary

Ink and page do source the rage
Like maiden hearts source wars we wage
Verbose or terse; in prose or verse
We seal the hearse with chandlery

Word and line can quicken time
Like intravenous poison
And life abruptly turns corrupt
From spreading truths empoisoned

Steel against the words we scribe
We've yet to find one antidote
Regardless, breaths of you survive
Within our twisted anecdotes

A Night at the Movies
2023

It starts beneath the marquee
One for you, and one for me
Keeping time in concession line
Make no concessions
Bathe in extra butter if you please
Grub in hand
       —Stubs in hand
Blindly brave aisles dim lit by LEDs
Kindly traverse an aisle full of knees
Favored seats found empty
Wrestle arms for armrest claims
Silence your tethers and
Let previews predict your future nights
Jaw-hinges work in projector light
Popcorn crunch crisp in open-chewing mouths
The biggest screen wide awake
Moving pictures on display
A narrative on lighted screen
What dramas will there play?

Feature Presentation
2021

I think you should cut it

What?

I think you should cut your hair.
I think it would look nice if it were
Short and Cropped

Don't be ridiculous!

Really!

Really?

You have very boyish features, y'know?

What's that supposed to mean?

Exactly how it sounds
You have very boyish features, and
I think you should cut your hair.
I could almost love a woman like that.

Almost?

Yes, well…
…

…

Well, why don't you cut your hair?

Why would I?

You have boyish features too, don't you?
You are a Man after all.

Are you sure?
Oh, come on!

Why would I cut my hair?
You like me with my hair long
Nails decorated
Besides, I have girlish features too

Like what?

My eyelashes, for one
My full lips, and high cheek bones

Oh yes, and a strong jaw
How Girlish *you appear.*

Don't laugh!
I do have a few girlish features.
Well, of course you do when you paint it on that way.

Don't sass!
You like my face painted,
And my hair long
And my decorated nails!
A lot of women models share these same features—
The jaw
The cheekbones.

Maybe it's just that they have boyish features too!

Or maybe it's just that some *boys* have *girlish* features.

Yes, well...

...

Who are we to say?

Your Age Now
2021

If I was your age now
Why, I'd kiss a boy like you

Like me?

Just like you.
If your chocolate eyes invite me to.
I'd kiss your supple lips
Sweet caress with fingertips
Why, if I was your age now
All the things that I would do.

Well, what more then?
Tell me more!

If I was your age now, I might murder in a dress
And once the pigs are summoned, greet them sweetly to confess,
But, of course, they'd never take me with my lashes long and low
For I'd quickly then convince them to pretermit what they know.

And how?

And how!

No, but how?

 Don't you know?
All dishonest men are privy to the selves they never show.

Oh, I do know.

I thought so.

We all know!

The First Curiosity
2020

Proof of guilt was hidden there,
She couldn't see it then, through the shambles of her own
But proof was there, even then, lodged in Adam's throat
The first bite of an apple from Eden

The first curiosity was not for the apple,
But Adam's for the Lotus.
What is it to blossom in the spring
To have silken petals kissed by drops of early morning dew?

Adam glances as Eve prances round, and round the apple tree
Legs stretch from her flower like stem-stalks to root in garden soil
The first bite lodges deep in Adam's throat
He envies her this beauty.

The way her hair rides the wind, he thinks, and twirls like ribbon
Her voice rising in playful chirps, harmonizing with birds
The way apple blossoms fall for her,
Surf the crest of her breast, or scuttle down her arching spine

He called to her, then, and tossed the apple.
"Lay with me here," he beckoned
The serpent peered from beneath him
Temptation had her then.

Woman I
2020

Place her up above
Just out of reach; near enough
To admire from far.

A picture of grace
A regal composition
She is a sculpted

Goddess of mankind
And all of their hearts alike
She buds like white rose,

Magnolia flowers
And lavender stalks in spring.
Steaming to seduce

Awash in spring baths
Soaking in mysterium
Dripping coy droplets

Strength cascades like silk
Along her rippling frame
Hair soaked in wisdom

Sunlight rides her curves
Glistening and glowing gold
Treasure her as such

Herald her as queen
Eyes pierce veils held before her
Secrets flock to ears

She wafts deception
Away with a Royal wave
A kiss from blessed

Lips trace lucky trails
On virgin foreheads. Aspire
To be a Woman.

The Gash
2021

A man thinks he might invest in
The Gash,
But what is a wound that doesn't
Bleed with the moon?

A phantom Gash, perhaps,
Suffering instead from
Phantom pains of
That thing.

This thing is a burden to the man,
But it belongs to him
Inherently.
Still he finds it strange.

It serves no purpose for this man.
He puts it to no good use.
He thinks he might invest
In the Gash.

It does sound grotesque,
"The Gash,"
But what is the organ without the womb;
Without fertile tubes,

And the bleeding with the moon?
He thinks he is underserving
Man has paid no dues
Man is no woman

But he longs to be

And, so he thinks
He might
Invest
In the gash.

Woman II
2022

So, this is the touch of a Woman,
Soft-skinned
Tender breast cupped in a possessing hand
The budding flesh
Protruding nipple indurated,
The sigh...
My own.

Divine, the sacred timekeeper
Hips convex below
Tick-ling hands
Nails tracing
Tremors chasing
Grip-holds like barrel waves
Alongside a buttoned beach
Entrenched by the abdomen
Sun-tanning
Torso spilling sands
Breath's dancing with the wind
Minutes metered in ocean swell.

Robots & Aliens
2017

Would you ever marry a robot?
If they were the baddest bitch
Ass is thick
Clean teeth and passionate
With a maddening sense
For when you're doing wrong
And a penchant
For always making sure you're getting all the attention
They draw the attention
Speaking up at all the events and
Throttle the tension
Makes it rise and fall, a magician
A mathematician
A scientist when they're in the kitchen
A therapist for all your perils.
And they're going to fix them
They'll be given you distance
Space to grow and exist in
Throws it down in the kitchen
I had to say it again
In the bedroom a vixen
Lingerie on the floor
Come here Mista-Misses Robot let me love you some more

Imagine spousing up an Alien
One who flew here from mars
Such a hand around the house and takes charge
Got a knack for showing off, riding round in big cars
Never not making that money and the probe is on large
They'll stay posted on guard, the protectors of your heart

Clipped Wings

See their glow-up in the star-light, Modern beauty off the charts
You see, the thing about love is that it stretches so far
Could you even love a human?
Should we show you where to start?
It's high time the writers drafted up some new fables
So, we can show them what the truth is once you've cut the label
It doesn't matter what nation you come from,
The color of your skin
Who you choose to love, trust, fuck, or call your friend
What you watch on the TV or play back in your ear
NUAM
Play that shit back with no fear!
I don't want to hear no moaning and griping about the make-up on
    my face
What gives you the right to make us feel out of place?
This is just as much our world as it ever was yours
We've been kings, slaves, and soldiers
Fighting in your wars
Servicing your stores
No one knows the true creator, but we are all the same creation
Now be a decent human being and stop all that hating.
This world is ours too and you'd best not forget it
Now, Mista-Misses Alien
Come on and get it!

Fruits & Flowers
2018

Roses are red
If violets are blue, who the fuck named them violets?
Oranges are Orange
Eating Bananas is provocative.

The Feels
2018

I feel it most when the sun is shining
Warm wind, and beads of sweat forming at my hairline
When I smell pollen on the air, or salted ocean spray,
Feel snow, and fog clinging to finer hairs on my arms and legs
It spreads within me, gassing me until the tank is full
With purple, pink, and fire lined clouds
I feel it and it is profound

I feel it all when the gravel, pebbles, sand,mud, grass, and clay
Crunches, grinds, shifts, squishes, bends, and molds beneath my
feet
When the wind whips around caressing bare skin
Tugging at my clothes, and lifting me to a climax
Of the senses.

It is astounding and euphoric when I feel it
At the tips of each limb
Tickling at my nape
Burning in the lobe of each ear
Pooling in the corners of my eyes,
And feathering the very tip of my nose—
A-Choo!
Bless up
I feel it most
It, he, she, them, we individual, and we in unison
When my soul reaches out to a tear-soaked frown,
Cowers away from a furious scowl
Or is as still as the quaint melancholy of overcast
I feel it all so greatly!
It is the unyielding glory of God,
The powerful pull of the Universe,

The overwhelming weight of Father Time,
Humble and humbling hands of Mother Nature.
It is all the proof that I need that I have survived deaths temptations.
I feel it,
Entirely alive.

Bucolic Charm
2020

It certainly has its charm:
The humbling storm clouds encroaching on green and yellow skies,
An adrenaline-fueled race away from—or towards—warned of
    tornados
A dewy petrichor from fresh rain after a long, dry summer.

It charms with undiluted evening sounds,
Echoing crickets, and wind in the tall grass,
A mothers wooden chimes hanging from the porch
It certainly charms
But does it romance like The City?

Metropolitan

2019

16 pair firmly planted
Among plenty more in this large tin can
Hinged to another, and several more others
We sisters and brothers journey on

In underground tunnels
A maze of rebellious painting on walls
Braced for the fall on these labor worn tracks,
Unreliable paths that lead us astray

Broken trains on dilatory schedules
Pounded pavement beneath rushing feet
Tunneling always into and out of
Like ants in this cavernous underground

Marching together up into daylight
From tunnel ends to towering jungle
Valleys of stone, glass, and steel
Where millions march side by side

A lonely collective in a monstrous city
Lovelorn, and weary from a sleepless spell
Even at night we tunnel through hell
Where the damned scream their cursed lament.

New York to the New Yorkers:
A Love Letter
2021

You're a real fuckin' pain, you know that?

Everyday
Up in the morning
Pounding the pavement
Sounding your horns
Enthralled in the hustle
(Don't mistake me, I don't knock it)
Injecting yourselves like speed into the veins of my underground
So that you can shoot up town for some late-night cabal
Dim lit debauchery in subbasement speaks
And the endless revolution against Blue in our streets
I stand with you
But you're a pain
It's no wonder I never fuckin' sleep.

And what do I do as I lay awake?
Listen to the endless rumble of above ground trains
Transporting you through synapse to the nerves of my being
Listen to maddening artists prophecy their greatness to
Maddening artists who drink to a self-perceived inadequacy.
I sing along to the subway song
Peddle my wares to the track rats as a songstress in a jazz club
Pours her soul into a microphone, singing of vagabond blues in
    that old New York
Where you repaint diluted stars with a fractured disco moon.

As I lay awake,
Day in and day out
Hearing testimony of this great city
I scoff at what I'd be without you

The New Yorkers
You're a real fuckin' pain
But at least you aren't tourists.

Life Doesn't Frighten Me
2021

No Longer a fear
But much more a knowing
A time-lapsed growing
The hand I've stopped showing
On rapid water flowing, it's an automated rowing
Counter-tide, Up stream
A white knuckled grip the dream

No longer a fear
But a steamboat whistle
Mickey mouse on the swivel
Eyes shut to the drivel
An ear to ear smiling at the would-be beguiling
Up the skirt, hook and pull
Mallets played on tooth of bull

No longer a fear
But a flickering desire
A single flame fire
Enough heat to perspire
A finger tracing embers, chasing frost in late December
Burning parallel to spine
Whiskey neat and Brandywine

This life, it doesn't frighten me.
I do not care at all.

No longer a caring
But an open oversharing
All temptation and daring
And baseless war declaring

A sought-after fight on a celebration night
Smiles through a busted lip
Savoring the bloody drip

No longer a caring
But a flippant rebuttal
The shoulder shrugging shuffle
Dulcet speech gone guttural
An anything but subtle childish splashing in a puddle.
A revelation made in spite
Tantrum thrown in sheer delight.

No longer a caring
Now a flagrant disavowing
A worry-free endowment
¡Hola! Ça'va? and Ciao!
The painted upper brow on a chicken, pig, and cow
A turn at noncompliance
Meek becomes the giant.

True Colors
2022

These are the colors I was

Pure like full moonlight on rolling hills of snow
Spilled milk cascading over the countryside from some
      unseen bottle.
Soft as processed cotton,
I was the sugar cube that sweetened the bitterest of brews

An endless bound between the horizons of imaginative spirit
Cold fingers on windswept winter shores
And the frigid waves that break themselves upon them

A putrid mucus spat upon the beauties of spring
Lemon custard paranoia in banana pudding halls
Yet still hopeful and optimistic on sundrenched mornings
A shade I should choose more often

These are the colors I was before
These are the ones I've become

Bruised and battered after the fight, but eager for another round
A berry bursting with ambition for noble pursuits
Gentle fresh clippings of lavender and lilac

Lively
Fresh cut grass staining favored jeans
The emerald mosaic of forest leaves
A budding rebirth
Breaking through the soil in search of brighter days
The lip stain lingering in hidden places
Impassioned and empowered in a strawberry slip

The surge of blood that blushes the cheek
In this one shade of me
Among many true colors

Speaking Plainly
2021

That is to say that in this one I have forgone the rhetoric,
Or done the best I can

Day 5
And this quarantine has offered me a healthier reflection than the
first, I hope
Three hours a day sitting at the keys.
Sometimes playing.
Sometimes sitting.
At least one hour of reading.
And I pass the rest with immeasurable paces back and forth in my
Covid hotel room
Short bursts of gaming on my PlayStation
Doom scrolling.
Ignoring texts and having texts ignored.
Amorous praises from a man I've never met before
But he swears that I'm the one, and he's been chasing for a year.
The only one, he says, who has ever made him feel this way.
I don't remember trying.
This feels like 19 all over again.
"Oh, how the tables turn, and cookies crumble to the floor."
Right?
He tells me I'm the reason for his sexuality
"Only you."
He doesn't understand the insult.
I suggest that I am a catalyst for a thing that was already there.
Hopefully next role is boyfriend
[sic]
Hard swallow.
It feels like everything I've asked for, yet nothing that I want.
He asks me out for drinks when I'm better.
Only time will tell.

This quarantine has given me a healthier contemplation
I hope
I'm contemplative of things both near and far from the heart
Things said to me
                    By me
                        About me
Things said to others
                    By others
                        About others
I never claim innocence—none of us ever are,
But maybe it's time to alter the approach
Maybe it is time to step away from the altar
Or nearer to it.
I contemplate God, or any idea of a higher power, as the complete
antithesis of Ego
But that is just my belief
You make your own
I contemplate humanity
This is nothing new except that now I contemplate it with Jennifer
Melfi and Tony Soprano
And a therapist of my own.
I contemplate death
I think about this trend that seems to exist to feign it.
"We're all dead."
"We are all already dead."
I used to participate in it…
I still do occasionally.
Nihilistic bullshit.
As if we're just a bunch of zombies milling about the surface of
the earth feeding off each other, and the planet, in the worst ways
possible
It may not be the furthest cry from the truth, but we are not dead
We play at it like dogs, but we are human
We are contemplating humanity, remember?
Foolishly eager to set ourselves apart from other animals

Clipped Wings

But our hearts also bleed
Our lungs also breath
All it takes is a little bit of resolve to pick yourself up from the floor
and live
For fuck's sake
Break the complacency
It's not a superpower, it's a willpower
We're all dead
The implication is a disrespect to those dead and dying
Humans don't play dead except in the interest of self-preservation.
In wartime, or experiences of extreme physical abuse
And if this is war, which it very well may be
Consider victory requiring a more proactive approach
If only to say we kept fighting until the end.